PATHWAYS TO PURPOSE

FEATHERWORKS
PUBLICATIONS

TAMPA

PATHWAYS TO PURPOSE

RITES OF PASSAGE
COMPANION GUIDE

SONYA D. FERREIRA

Pathways to Purpose

Copyright © 2025 by Sonya D. Ferreira

Published by Featherworks Publications

Cover and book designed by David Ferreira

For more information:
Featherworks Publications
Tampa, FL

Ferreira, Sonya D.
Pathways to purpose / Sonya D. Ferreira

ISBN 979-8-9905804-3-5 (Paperback)
ISBN 979-8-9905804-4-2 (eBook)

Library of Congress Control Number: 2025950059

First Edition

Printed in the United States of America.

"True humility and fear of the Lord lead to riches, honor, and long life. Corrupt people walk a thorny, treacherous road; whoever values life will avoid it. Direct your children onto the right path, and when they are older, they will not leave it."
Prov 22:4-6 (NLT)

DEDICATION

To the men of standard in my life:

David,
My steadfast husband and leader
on this incredible journey of life,
whose strength and loyalty
continually inspire those around him.

Elijah and Ephraim,
Beloved sons,
each embarking on your own unique paths
while finding your courage and hope to walk out
all of God's plans for you.

May you always pursue your journey
with heart and valor,
embracing each rite of passage
with the knowledge that you are loved deeply
and supported unconditionally.

CONTENTS

HOW TO USE THIS GUIDE

Welcome to this pilgrimage of discovery and maturation! *Pathways to Purpose* is a *Companion Guide* designed to be a resource through your personal journey of revelation and connection to practical application of principles found in the book, ***Rites of Passage: Raising Sons to be Men of Standard***. To maximize the guidebook's effectiveness, read the book first or along with this guide, as it provides the foundation for understanding the significance of rites in the lives of our children, especially boys and young men transitioning into adulthood. It also cultivates the groundwork for leadership development in future generations and those we influence or impact.

The core message of Rites of Passage is focused on developing leaders who lead with character and that is not limited to boys and young men. In fact, the emphasis is on the importance of community and leveraging influence, along with raising children to be wise leaders with standards who are committed to serving their families, communities, and society.

This guide can be used individually, but it is more powerful when paired with discussion, either with a mentor, friend, or in a group setting. By engaging with others on their journey, we participate in collaborative discussions, deepen our insights, and increase the potential for life application of the material by learning from others. In using this guide, I suggest following a pattern such as the one below.

1. **Beginning with a quiet moment**: Set aside a few minutes of intimacy and remove the distractors. Prepare your heart and mind to listen and receive wisdom. The goal of this process is not just knowledge or education, but transformational thinking that produces a new way of living.

2. **Discussing each chapter of the workbook**: Talk about the key points, ask questions, and personalize the discussion to your life journey and family. Wisdom is gained through application so don't just listen and talk, walk out the principles.

3. **Reflecting after each session**: Each chapter has a unique life focus that correlates to the principles found in the book. Take time to ponder, dig deeper, and let the insights from the material stir your heart. Embrace the work of developing patterns, breaking habits, and adjusting behaviors that hinder progress. Let this time reveal areas that need nurturing or people you may need to nurture.

4. **Meditating between sessions**: Between individual sessions or group discussions, contemplate different parts of the material that resonate with you. Be still and consider how you can integrate those insights into your life to help you grow in understanding.

5. **Documenting insights**: We remember, or remind ourselves, of the things we write down. So write it down…track what you sensed in the reading, discussion or a particular moment then invite God to give more revelation by journaling about it. Writing will enable you to remember and reflect on your experiences for future reference.

6. **Seeking accountability and counsel**: You should trust the wisdom of your mentors, peers, or people that support you in life and during this journey. They may see things about you that you cannot see about yourself. Permit trusted confidantes to provide valuable encouragement in this maturation process.

In essence, this guide helps you seek, refine, and broaden your life perspective. It is a tool for applying the teachings in the Rites of Passage book that allows you to customize them into meaningful ways of impact for those in your sphere of influence. Reading *Rites of Passage: Raising Sons to Be Men of Standard* with the *Pathways to Purpose* guide is essential for anyone committed to producing leaders through a structured, values-based process focused on growth. Here's why both resources are relevant and important:

1. Holistic Development

The book provides a strong foundation in principles, values, and responsibilities necessary for raising children to be responsible stewards and honorable adults. The guide reinforces these teachings by offering practical exercises, reflection points, and applications that solidify the lessons.

2. Engaged Learning & Application

Simply reading about the principles of adulthood or leadership is not enough; applying them is a gamechanger. This guide equips parents, mentors, community or group leaders, and children to actively engage with the discussion of maturing through self-reflection, goal setting, and prompts to make the learning process interactive and personal.

3. Guided Mentorship & Accountability

If you don't know where to start, the guide serves as a reference to engage in structured mentorship. It provides discussion points and activities to address challenges, memorialize special occasions, and help internalize lessons that can be transformed into insights that are practiced in the life of leaders of integrity and responsibility.

4. Cultural & Spiritual Foundation

The book lays a biblical and moral foundation for young men and women, while the guide helps instill these principles through practical application that provokes thinking critically about purpose, faith, and our roles in society in conjunction with spiritual and personal development.

5. Preparation for Adulthood

Becoming a man of standard requires intentionality. The Rites of Passage book gives a roadmap and the guide promotes active engagement in the rites, traditions, and ceremonies to equip young leaders with real-life skills fostering discipline, character, and respect.

6. Family & Community Involvement

Using both resources together cultivates family bonds and partnership. Parents, mentors, and faith leaders can work through the material, reinforcing the idea that adulthood is not a solo journey but one supported by a strong community.

Call to Action: Developing a Generation of Leaders

How do we develop character in our children and those we lead? By making it a priority and being intentional. Following the lessons in *Pathways to Purpose*, helps children and young adults understand leadership. The combination of vision-setting, structured learning, real-world application, mentorship, and accountability facilitates the environment individuals need to matriculate into responsible, value-driven leaders who make a meaningful, positive impact on those around them.

For those serious about raising strong, principled leaders, reading *Rites of Passage: Raising Sons to Be Men of Standard* is just the beginning. The real transformation happens when children and their mentors actively partake with the *Pathways to Purpose*, applying the lessons in real time and positioning our future generations to lead well. Enjoy the journey!

For speaking engagements or more information on sharing Rites of Passage principles, please connect with the author on EmissaryWay.com.

A MESSAGE TO PARENT-LEADERS

In her book, The Garden Within, Dr. Anita Phillips acknowledges the impact of the 2020 Covid pandemic on celebrating special milestones and ceremonial moments that "entwine us in relationship and in community."[1] My son Elijah was in the class of 2020 cohort and he was marked by this crisis. This work reflects all those, like him, who had to pursue another pathway to purpose.

As a mother of sons, I often find myself pondering the journey of raising boys into men—men of strength, wisdom, and unwavering integrity. It is a sacred responsibility, one that requires intention, guidance, and the collective effort of a community that values leadership rooted in faith and character.

In a world that challenges the very foundation of moral leadership, we must be deliberate about nurturing future generations of responsible leaders, our children. Parents are leaders of leaders, and we cannot afford to leave their growth to chance. Instead, we must equip them with the resources to become the leaders we desire to see in our families, communities, and the world.

This is why the moral leadership principles outlined in **Rites of Passage: Raising Sons to be Men of Standard** are so critical. We don't get a second chance to raise our children, so it is imperative to be engaged the first time. The book identifies nine passageways that individuals navigate to become stalwart, mature leaders. These passages are not just theoretical ideologies; they are lived experiences that help our children and young adults develop the proper attitudes and behaviors essential to progressing through their life journey.

This guide was written in response to the question, "How do I make the Rites of Passage principles relevant, practical, and real in my life with each of my children?" Each chapter in **Pathways to Purpose** serves as a reflection point for flexible conversations between parents/children, guardians, mentors, and community leaders. It opens the thought process to identify and mark significant milestones in the process of maturation. Let's be intentional to create moments, ceremonies, and traditions that shape the hearts and minds of future leaders. Whether

---

[1] Phillips, Anita. (2023). The Garden Within. Nelson Books.

it is acknowledging their achievements, instilling responsibility, or guiding them through challenges, every step we take with those we influence matters. These rites of passage are more than events; they are the building blocks of lifelong character that leaves a legacy.

Together, we can raise the standard for leadership by calling them to live with integrity and serve their communities. In their seasons of preparation, we lead and train them to walk in victory on the road ahead because…it is their time to rise!

Let's Pray:
Lord, thank you for the privilege to be parents, leaders, and mentors in our homes and communities. Remind us of the awesome responsibility to serve and lead well while committing to personal growth so we can help others develop too. In Jesus Name, Amen!

INTRODUCTION

How did I discover the value of Rites of Passage ceremonies? I did not discover it. It discovered me. The significance was revealed during a period of my life when I was separated from my family serving on a military tour. I am a mother of two sons. My elder son's 16th birthday was approaching, and I was struggling to find ways to validate him during this time of transition. I felt the strong impression to honor him beyond a birthday celebration; the moment needed was to be a commemoration. A recognition of milestones achieved and equipping for the journey ahead. He needed to be affirmed and called up into manhood, into leadership. What a thought to drop on me… suddenly!

As I pondered this notion, I realized I never had that level of affirmation as a child and neither did my husband. There was no calling us up to adulthood; we simply made mistakes then struggled to learn and grow through them. I wanted a better way of raising our sons based on standards and I do not believe I am alone in that desire as a parent. By God's grace, I encountered vessels throughout my life who showed me what it meant to lead others well, how to parent better, and how to serve effectively in my community.

In our digital world, many teenagers grow up with the same questions and voids I had. Some are deprived of the social skills to form genuine human connections even as adults. Technology can be beneficial but left unchecked, our societies will suffer from a lack of commitment in families, relationships, and communities. When circumstances are challenging, inconvenient, or unpleasant people just "check out" and move on to the next headline; however, maturation cannot happen without overcoming adversity. We grow stronger in our challenges and children learn to overcome trials if they stay in the test long enough to conquer it.

A hard truth remains: in this life all of us will suffer pain. We will go through troubling times of our own making and the making of others. None of these trials can be avoided in the process of matriculation into adulthood but they can be leveraged for those seeking a life of purpose. We cannot spend our lives running from challenges or wishing them away. Instead, we must learn how to stand firm during them.

Through my time of reading, reflecting, and meditating on godly principles, I began to pray for understanding of the root issues manifesting in societies that result in poor leadership in our homes, communities, and nations. I wondered what I could do to impact such lofty issues. What do I have in my hands or my sphere of influence? The answer became very clear: my children. My sons are gifts and the way I parent impacts the type of men, husbands, fathers, and leaders they could become. From this premise, the seed for Rites of Passage was implanted in my heart.

I had a vision for raising sons to be leaders but no roadmap or plans. The details came later through more time in contemplation and prayer. Symbolically, I climbed to my watchtower, as a mother, interceding on behalf of children globally. As I looked to see what would be revealed, I stood on guard patiently waiting and listening to discern the message the Lord was speaking to my heart. I wanted to know His answer and how He would respond to my concerns as a mother and a leader.

I prayed for the nations and the impact on our children. I prayed God would be merciful to them knowing we are amid spiritual warfare with attacks on marriages and families, attacks on our minds and values, attacks in schools and places of worship, attacks on moral leadership and government systems around the world.

Yes, parent-leaders we are at war with external and internal forces fighting for the hearts and souls of our children, and the adversary takes no prisoners. My enemy, your enemy, and the enemy of our children has no code of conduct. He does not play by any rules of engagement and he does not give mercy. His intent is to utterly destroy families and communities, pitting one group of individuals against another causing division and inciting divisive schemes that influence children from a young age. He is ruthless but I am encouraged because in the end believers win! In the interim, we wrestle against forces in this journey called life.

In scripture, Ephesians 6:10-18 reminds us we are in spiritual warfare throughout the earth. The Message Translation reads: "And that about wraps it up. God is strong, and he wants you strong. So, take everything the Master has set out for you, well-made weapons of the best materials. And put them to use so you will be able to stand up to everything the devil throws your way. This is no weekend war that we'll walk away from and forget about in a couple of hours. This is for keeps, a life-or-death fight to the finish against the devil and all his angels. Be prepared. You're up against far more than you can handle on your own. Take all the help you can get, every weapon God has issued so that when it's all over but the shouting you'll still be on your feet."[2]

My sons are a part of this world just like your sons and daughters. Parents need community to thrive as parent-leaders in our technology-based, open access world. For parents to fight against forces of evil and strategies of deception, we cannot be ignorant or passive about spiritual warfare. I was inspired to write this message to help other parents understand the responsibility and consequences for parent-leaders. Rites of Passage is a message and a call to action for parents and all leaders to take back parental influence and steward our responsibility for raising leaders in our communities.

Are you committed to raising the standard together?

[2] Peterson, Eugene. (2002). The Message: The Bible in Contemporary Language. NavPress.

-CHAPTER-
ONE

ENTER THE
RITES OF PASSAGE

Reflection Point: Your Plan or God's Plan?

If you were raised in certain cultural communities or religious groups, rites of passage may be familiar. However, for many people, these ceremonies remain an unknown concept. They were neither practiced nor taught in their childhood, leaving a gap in their understanding of the importance of structured transitions into adulthood. I did not grow up in a family that honored rites of passage ceremonies and neither did my peers. As a result, I missed the significance of this impartation and the intentional preparation it provides for life's transitions.

In much of American society, growing up is often defined simply by the passage of time—another birthday, another year—rather than by a guided process of maturation. Instead of being discipled through key stages of development, many young people navigate adulthood without the structure, wisdom, and support these moments offer. So, what can we do differently to bridge the gaps between childhood and adulthood, immaturity and maturity?

One beauty of a rites of passage ceremony lies in its preparation. It should make us reflect on the essential lessons, values, and traditions our children need to not only grow older but to truly mature into leaders. The faith, principles, and cultural heritage we pass on should be intentionally cultivated daily so the impact is evident in our children's development and those around us.

Routines can become mundane and easily overlooked, but pausing to acknowledge milestones is vital. Just as a toddler must learn the necessity of using the bathroom instead of a diaper, teenagers must understand how to transition into productive and responsible adults. While bodily functions should develop automatically, proper training ensures children learn to manage them appropriately. In the same way, emotional, mental, and spiritual development do not occur randomly—parent-leaders must engage this process with intention.

Potty training is not just for the parents' convenience in avoiding diaper changes; it is for the child's growth and independence. We recognize that a teenager in diapers would be entirely different from a newborn in diapers—an unnatural and concerning situation. Likewise, a teenager who is not learning proper emotional, mental, and spiritual development is just as dependent as a toddler resisting potty training. Despite the toddler's resistance and parent frustrations, we persist in teaching them, believing they will eventually grasp the concept. We remain consistent in our training because we understand its value and benefits.

Parents cannot afford to give their maturing children any less attention and guidance than they would toddlers. Although our children's needs evolve over time, they still require instruction, support, and accountability as they transition into adulthood. Rites of passage ceremonies serve as powerful growth markers, celebrating moments of elevation while ensuring they step into their new roles with clarity, purpose, and responsibility.

A similar principle applies to adults we lead and interact with in our families, workplaces, or communities. To be productive adults, they may need guidance in specific places that are underdeveloped.

Make it Practical
Rites of Passage ceremonies mark defining moments of transition, both individually and within families and communities. These ceremonies should be intentionally designed to recognize shifts in perspective, posture, or responsibility, calling individuals to a higher standard of living through clearly communicated principles.

Identifying a Rite of Passage Event

1. **Reflect on Significant Moments**
   Consider key life events that have been meaningful to you and your family. For individuals, these might include milestone birthdays, baptisms, commencements, new business ventures, or weddings. For families, significant anniversaries, holidays, or long-standing traditions may serve as ideal opportunities.

2. **List Defining Moments**
   Identify and document moments that had a profound impact on the person you want to honor and their family. Take time to pray, reflect, and journal about why these moments were significant.

3. **Identify 1-2 Key Rites of Passage Events**
   To maintain the sacredness of the experience, select one or two significant Rite of Passage events to celebrate at key times of transition. Intentionally limiting the quantity of events ensures a meaningful and well-prepared celebration rather than hosting a series of transactional events.

4. **Gather Family Input**
   Once the event is chosen, discuss your ideas with family members and close friends to gain insight and perspective. Understanding their experiences can help shape the ceremony to be more authentic and impactful.

5. **Set a Date and Plan Logistically**
   When ready, choose a date and mark it on your calendar. Select a location that aligns with the significance of the event. Create a budget and set a timeline with key milestones to track your progress. Early communication with ceremony participants about their roles and your expectations is essential. Send out a save the date announcement.

6. **Make It Authentic and Meaningful**
   Ensure the ceremony reflects your family's values, faith, culture, or traditions. Incorporate relevant rituals, words of affirmation, or symbolic acts that reinforce the transition being celebrated. If needed, consider consulting an event specialist for guidance.

Next Steps

If you are serious about celebrating with a Rite of Passage event, what will you do within the next 30 days after you complete this guide? Set a goal, act, and create a memorable experience that honors growth and transition in a purposeful way for all participants.

-CHAPTER-
TWO

PASSAGE OF UNCERTAINTY

Reflection Point: Anchoring Identity in a Shifting World

Without the stories of the day, the ever-changing news cycle, and shifting cultural trends—do you know what you believe in?

What about your children? What shapes and defines them?

Are their beliefs rooted in something enduring, or do they fluctuate with the times?

Rites of passage have long played a crucial role in shaping values, marking transitions from one stage of life to another. These experiences provide a sense of belonging, purpose, and clarity—grounding individuals and helping them stand firm amid the ebb and flow of societal changes.

We must know what we stand for and what's a solid foundation that remains unshaken in moments of joy and times of sorrow. We must be secure in our convictions, guided by principles rather than popular opinion. Whether in a crowd or in solitude, your hope should not be predicated on trends but in an unchanging source.

If we do not firmly know what we believe, how can we guide others, particularly children, to walk with faith? Their sense of worth can be nurtured through meaningful rites of passage ceremonies rooted in purpose-driven, eternal values.

Make It Practical
Consider the following questions and write down your responses. What is your source? Where do you place your confidence?

Share your insights with a trusted confidante involved in the event planning.

Has the guest of honor displayed vulnerability or revealed uncertainties about their transition? Consider ways to help them in the transition?

What are their apprehensions, concerns? Will the event address and affirm those areas?

Is the event focused on a theme, and does it seek to convey a message?

Ceremonies can be costly, what do you hope to communicate/ accomplish through this investment? What will a successful event look like? What is your budget?

-CHAPTER-
THREE

PASSAGE OF BECOMING

Reflection Point: Don't Take Gifts to the Grave - Die Empty

It has been said that the greatest collection of untapped potential lies in the graveyard. How tragic is that! The thought of all those hopes and dreams left unfulfilled with talent buried in those who never became all they were meant to be.

Life demands reflection—an honest examination of who we are, who we want to become, and what impact we wish to leave behind. By contemplating the end, we gain clarity on how to navigate the journey in between. To truly live with purpose, we must align our lives with core principles and values that shape our decisions, behaviors, and priorities.

Becoming is not passive; it is an intentional pursuit. It requires understanding our motivations, the internal forces that propel us forward or hold us back. When left unexamined, people drift through life aimlessly, forfeiting the rich harvest their lives were designed to produce. When we embrace discovery and purpose, we step into the fullness of our calling, ensuring that our gifts do not go to the grave unused.

Make It Practical

What does the guest of honor value in life? Have they talked about their purpose?

What principles and priorities matter to them based on how they invest their time, talents, and treasure?

What are the guests of honor's career, academic, personal, professional, health or spiritual goals? How can this information be expressed and affirmed in the Rites of Passage celebration?

-CHAPTER-
FOUR

PASSAGE OF NAMING

Reflection Point: The Power of a Name, The Weight of Reputation

Everyone has a name, and often, a reputation that follows it. A name is given at birth, chosen without our input, yet it becomes a lifelong identifier. Unless changed through deliberate effort, we carry our names with us through every stage of life. No legal or business transactions can be completed without a name, it is essential to our identity and existence in society.

Names matter. They can evoke power, privilege, and authority shaping first impressions before a word is spoken. Over time, a name becomes intertwined with a reputation, possibly a badge of honor or a burden to bear. A name can symbolize family heritage, cultural significance, or personal meaning making it a source of pride and tradition.

Because of this, choosing a name wisely is no small responsibility. More than just letters and sounds, names carry weight. They reflect character, values, and legacy. Just as a name can open doors, it can also be tarnished by poor choices. It is up to each person to uphold the honor of their name, ensuring it remains a symbol of integrity and respect for generations to come.

Make It Practical
What is the meaning of the guest of honor's name?

What is the origin of their family name? Does the place of origin have any special significance?

Are there other names or titles they identify with based on faith or culture?

How can this information be meaningfully highlighted in the Rites of Passage?

Parents of newborns:
How do you see your newborn child at 5, 15, and 25 years old? Do you see signs of their purpose and destiny?

Will the chosen name grow with your child and remain meaningful through each stage of life?

Does the name speak honor and respect to its bearer?

-CHAPTER-
FIVE

PASSAGE OF TRADITIONS AND CEREMONIES

Reflection Point: Significant Events are Significant

Rites of passage traditions and ceremonies serve as powerful markers of transformation, anchoring individuals in their faith, relationships, and identity. These rituals not only celebrate significant moments but also impart essential values, ensuring that meaning and purpose are passed down through generations.

My sons like the DreamWorks movie, The Prince of Egypt. It is a tale of two brothers called to divergent destinies based on who they serve. One was born a Hebrew, among captive people, the other was born as a prince of Egypt but both were meant to be leaders of their respective people. The movie portrays their brotherly love followed by their adversarial relationship after one brother, Moses, discovers his true identity as a Hebrew.

Ultimately, Moses rejects the traditions of Egypt and is chosen to lead his people through a profound rite of passage recorded in the book of Exodus. Before Moses leads the Hebrew people on their miraculous departure from 400 years of slavery in Egypt, they are commanded to prepare a specific meal to observe the first Passover. The Passover was a symbolic meal that foreshadowed the death of Jesus Christ, the Lamb of God, and affirmed Israel's covenant with Yahweh who provides deliverance and protection. Before their exodus from Egyptian slavery, they were instructed to cover the doorposts of their homes with the blood of a lamb signaling God's death angel to "pass over" their homes and sparing the lives of their firstborn children and livestock.

Since that first Passover in Egypt, Jewish believers have faithfully observed God's salvation through an annual Feast of the Passover. Millennia have passed, yet this holy festival remains a cornerstone of Jewish identity—a cultural tradition and a sacred memorial to divine deliverance. It is a time for families to gather over a meal, recount the story of their ancestors, and instill faith and heritage in the next generation.

Some modern disciples of Jesus Christ, though not Jewish, also celebrate Passover by recognizing its deeper meaning in light of Christ's sacrifice for all people. Jesus of Nazareth is called the "Lamb of God" because His death provided salvation and freedom to everyone who accepts Him. This connection between Jewish culture and Christian faith highlights the importance of remembering and honoring milestones in a way that strengthens spiritual and cultural foundations.

Culture and tradition provide context for events we deem significant. They deepen our loyalty and reinforce the reasons we celebrate. It is crucial to join our traditions with meaning, ensuring they are not another party or annual gathering. Our children must understand the "why" behind the celebration, and as parents, we bear the responsibility of passing this knowledge on to them (Joshua 4:5-8).

Beyond religious observances, every family has opportunities to establish meaningful rites of passage. Parents should seek ways to recognize and honor their children with purpose. Events like a milestone birthday, anniversaries, or important accomplishments are meant to be recognized because these moments, both great and small, serve as life markers. Some milestones are "big rocks," such as graduating from college, getting married, or embracing a new faith commitment. Others are "smaller stones," like persevering through a challenging school year or completing a demanding sports season. Some milestones are life-altering, such as navigating the tragic loss of a loved one. Every significant moment holds the potential to teach future generations life lessons that shape character and values.

By establishing meaningful rites of passage and putting practices that honor these principles in motion, we affirm the growth and development of our children and those around us. We recognize their journey, guide them through transitions, and equip them with a strong sense of identity. Just as the Passover unites generations in remembrance and faith, our family traditions and ceremonies serve as enduring pillars of encouragement carrying lessons from the past to illuminate the way forward.

Make it Practical

Is there an event that has historical, cultural, or spiritual meaning that makes it fitting to be a Rite of Passage ceremony?

Who is the intended audience beyond the guest of honor? Who else would benefit?

What are the most important factors in making this event happen for you/your family? (Time Commitment, Planning Ability, Financial Limitations, etc.)

Are there any deal breakers for the Rite of Passage event? How do you mitigate those issues?

-CHAPTER-
SIX

PASSAGE OF IDENTITY

Reflection Point: You Are Known

People are created in the image of God but they choose how they want to live. Understanding identity is foundational to walking in purpose, and Exodus chapters 1-3 provide a powerful backdrop for this truth. The journey of Moses exemplifies the process of discovering your identity and stepping into divine calling. Moses was born into a perilous time when the Egyptian Pharaoh decreed the murder of all Hebrew baby boys. Yet, by God's providence, Moses was spared—hidden by his mother, then drawn from the water and adopted by Pharaoh's daughter. Though raised as an Egyptian prince, Moses first spent his early years under the care of his Hebrew mother, an experience that likely planted seeds about his identity.

By Exodus 3, Moses became a fugitive for killing an Egyptian in defense of a Hebrew slave. Fleeing to Midian, he embraced a new life as a shepherd but even in his wilderness, God—El Roi, the One who sees—had a plan. Through a burning bush encounter, God appointed Moses as a national leader and affirmed Moses by sharing divine truths about Himself.

1. **God is Holy**. Moses was instructed to remove his sandals because he stood on holy ground in the presence of Yahweh. (Exodus 3:5)

2. **God Reveals Himself**. He introduced Himself as "the God of your father, the God of Abraham, the God of Isaac, and the God of Jacob." God does not deceive or manipulate; He wants people to know and enjoy fellowship with Him. (Exodus 3:6a)

3. **God's Presence Exposes Truth**. Moses instinctively hid his face, recognizing his own human frailty in the light of God's holiness. (Exodus 3:6b)

4. **God Consecrates Whoever He Chooses**. God's presence transforms the ordinary or unclean into holy vessels fit for His service. He calls and makes leaders holy. (Exodus 3:14-15)

Growing up, I marveled at the story of Moses and how God used him to deliver Israel. Yet, one question remained: How did Moses respond to God so quickly with such reverence and obedience considering what God was asking Moses to do? Moses was born a Hebrew but raised as an Egyptian prince. Scripture does not detail his time with his mother, but we know she nursed him as a baby before he stayed in Pharaoh's household. Could it be that this brief period helped shape his identity in unseen ways? Despite years of Egyptian culture and influence, something in Moses' heart recognized the suffering of his Hebrew kin and Moses felt compelled to help. Later he encounters God at the burning bush and instinctively knew the God of his ancestors, not Egypt where he was raised, but the God of Israel. This suggests that the foundation laid in his early life was not erased by his royal upbringing and God was revealing more of His plan for Moses.

Moses' mother saw that he was special and hid him to preserve his life. Coming from the tribe of Levi—the priestly tribe—Moses carried a divine mandate of consecration. Could it be that God used his mother to imprint identity and purpose within him, even before he was aware of it? When he encountered Yahweh in the desert, maybe his spirit bore witness to the voice of his true God, leading to his quick surrender.

Our identity is established by God before we fully comprehend it. Like Moses, we may journey through seasons of uncertainty, but when we encounter the presence of God the truth of who we are in Him resonates deeply within us. We are not defined by our circumstances or upbringing, but by the One who calls us by name.

Make It Practical

As parents, do you believe we have a vital responsibility to speak identity into the lives of our children? How is it demonstrated in your family?

Even when children grow up, if they depart from their training, do you believe they have a beacon of hope implanted within them to guide them back to the voice of truth?

What can you do through a Rite of Passage to help your children realize their true identity, not the identity others place on them?

Are there specific pronouncements, blessings, or affirmations that could be delivered in a Rite of Passage event to strengthen the guest of honor?

What areas do you want to emphasis or memorialize during the ceremony? (i.e. family principles, memories, keepsake, traditions)

-CHAPTER-
SEVEN

PASSAGE OF CHARACTER AND INTEGRITY

Reflection Point: Integrity Never Goes Out of Style

It is interesting in today's time the default approach when faced with two poor choices has become, "Let's pick the best of the worst...the lesser of two evils." But is the best of the worst good? Perhaps it is time to reframe our perspective. Instead of settling for lesser evils, why not intentionally cultivate what is good and steadfastly resist what is evil?

Character, whether good or bad, is the result what we cultivate over time. A fundamental aspect of character is the consistent alignment of words with actions. No one builds a good reputation through routine lies or deceit. Instead, people of character practice speaking the truth, honoring their words and keeping commitments. They live with integrity.

The New Testament recounts multiple stories about a group of leaders known as the Pharisees (Matthew 15; Matthew 23:1-36). Though this group of religious leaders may have started their work with good intentions, they eventually succumbed to ego and self-ambitions. They were quick to accuse and condemn others without acknowledging their own faults. Their double standards held others accountable for rules the Pharisees could not uphold themselves. Jesus condemned this hypocrisy because true character and integrity are qualities God wants His people to possess. It is not about keeping up with the Kardashians or superficial appearances. God looks at our hearts - who we genuinely are on the inside.

Integrity is so vital that God explicitly included honesty as a key principle in His commandments – thou shall not lie. Scripture states that God hates a lying tongue (Proverbs 6:16-19). Throughout Psalms, Proverbs, and the New Testament dishonesty, deceit, and corruption are repeatedly condemned as destructive and unrighteous behaviors. Instead, we are commanded to live with integrity, generosity, and service in our communities.

One of the most impactful ways to pass on the values of character and integrity is through intentional affirmation of our children and those we influence. By upholding meaningful traditions, ceremonies, and life lessons leaders can instill nurturing attitudes, behaviors, and principles that serve as guiding lights for future generations. By teaching integrity in practical ways that align our life choices with proper actions, we provide an unwavering foundation—one that will sustain future generations.

Make It Practical
Anyone who spends significant time with you sees who you really are. Do you know your character strengths and limitations? What impact do they have on those around you?

How do you know your children or subordinates are internalizing the right values (passing the leadership test) at home, work, or school?

What encouragement is needed for them to embrace future roles and responsibilities?

What admonishment should be shared to keep them living a life of integrity?

-CHAPTER-
EIGHT

PASSAGE OF SUFFERING WITH GRATITUDE

Reflection Point: Trials Test All of Us

Few individuals have encountered suffering as profound as the trials Job experienced. His narrative serves as a testament to human resilience, humility, and unwavering faith amid staggering losses and tribulations. Job's life presents extreme contrasts. Initially, he was blessed abundantly then plunged into severe affliction but ultimately restored. This dramatic shift challenges our understanding of a benevolent God and prompts questions about His nature and the existence of divine goodness.

Yet, Job's experiences also provide valuable insights into divine intentions. God permits Satan, the adversary, to take away everything—Job's family, wealth, and health. His affliction was so severe that it altered his appearance and pushed him into despair even regretting his own birth. Despite this hardship, Job's trials refine his faith and deepen his understanding of God's character. Job's calamities underscore how suffering is an intrinsic part of human existence and he provides an example of how we can choose to respond. Job's life reveals two lessons:

1. **The Origin of Suffering**: Suffering is not intentionally inflicted by God but originates from God's enemy, Satan, who aims to undermine our faith in a just and loving God. Even in Job's trials, Satan operates under God's divine sovereignty, illustrating that nothing occurs beyond God's overarching authority. (Job 1:6-22)

2. **The Purpose of Divine Permittance**: Although God envisages a peaceful and prosperous life for humanity (as depicted in Genesis 1-2), human choices and actions introduced suffering into our world. The repercussions of these actions are irreversible and suffering often acts as a painful lesson that we need to change or make wiser choices in the future. God's allowance of suffering makes us confront the reality of free will and the significant consequences that accompany our freedom when not governed wisely. (Genesis 3)

It is common to accuse or blame in the face of suffering, especially when we feel we've done nothing wrong to cause it. However, we must recognize that our societal, familial, and personal choices along with the inherent presence of evil all contribute to pain and suffering throughout the world. Sometimes, as in Job's case, suffering arises without direct cause from our behaviors; it is a result of Satan's enmity towards God and people. Satan aims to discredit God by stealing hope, destroying dreams, and wreaking havoc to perpetuate divisiveness and chaos resulting in suffering among the righteous and the wicked.

Understanding and teaching our children about the nature of suffering is important for their spiritual maturity, emotional health, and resilience. When they recognize suffering does not signify divine neglect but a flawed world, they grow in understanding and empathy. When we deepen our comprehension of suffering, we build faith that not only endures hardships but matures us through them.

The human mind often struggles to grasp the full extent of the machinations of evil and the suffering it unleashes. One way people grapple with their understanding of evil behaviors is to label them as mental health issues. Bona fide mental health issues exist but not all evil behaviors arise from mental health concerns and to believe that narrative undermines individuals who are truly experiencing mental health challenges and doing good in their communities. The reality is people want to lessen the discomfort of living in a world with evil, so they rationalize it. It makes sense to deem evil behaviors we can't understand as a mental health issue rather than acknowledging evil forces are operating against us and in the world around us.

Since pain and suffering are inescapable, we must equip ourselves, our children, and those we lead to stand and persevere through challenges because suffering with gratitude, instead of bitterness, develops us. Without suffering, we could not fully experience gratitude, a vital part of resilient living in a world that has pain. God's undying love is demonstrated through Jesus Christ's suffering on the cross to save all humanity from eternal death. Ultimately, Job's journey illustrates how profound loss and suffering can still result in gratitude, wisdom, and enriched relationship with the God who saves.

Make It Practical
Do you have honest conversations about the difficulties your children face in life without trying to solve the issue or make it go away?

Have you had honest conversations with those in close relationships with you or people you lead/mentor? Do you allow others to process their painful experiences and grow?

Do you share your personal experiences of overcoming challenges with others?

In the Rites of Passage book, what passages resonate most with you and the guest of honor? How have those challenges impacted you and him/her?

How will this event pass on knowledge and strength to overcome future obstacles?

How will the event emphasis the benefits of growing from painful experiences and suffering with gratitude?

How can the event include suffering with gratitude in a personal, spiritual, and/or cultural context that encourages faith and resilience?

Next Step:
Acknowledge any area in your life that needs more fortification, healing, or closure.

Consider how embracing gratitude in times of suffering can change the perspective of suffering through a painful experience.

-CHAPTER-
NINE

PASSAGE OF GENERATIONAL COVENANT AND FAMILY RITES

Reflection Point: The Solitary Path to Passing the Mantle

Throughout history, the transfer of a generational mantle has shaped legacies that impact people, both positively and negatively. A legacy transcends material wealth or achievements; it encompasses the transmission of values, traditions, and responsibilities that forge paths for future generations. Legacy is the inheritance passed on to our successors to fulfill their destiny.

Before the events of Joshua chapter 5, the children of Israel were liberated from Egyptian bondage. Yet, their journey to the Promised Land was delayed in the wilderness by their discontentment, lack of faith, and disobedience. Consequently, all the adults who were delivered out of Egyptian captivity, except for Joshua and Caleb, perished in the wilderness. It was the demise of a generation who was unable or unwilling to embrace the promise of God. Standing on the cusp of their inheritance, their children, the next generation was now ready to fight for the land promised by God.

Prior to battle, they were required to engage in a significant rite of passage: circumcision (Joshua 5:2-7). This intentional and ceremonial act was more than a physical removal; it also symbolized a covenant with their God, Yahweh. In Jewish custom, the practice of circumcision was performed on the eighth day after birth (Genesis 17:12, Leviticus 12:3). The absence of circumcision for adult male children of Jewish descent raises some questions: Why did their parents and leaders of the community neglect to pass down this crucial part of their cultural heritage and spiritual covenant? Why did these young men reach adulthood without undergoing this sacred practice? What distractors stop parent-leaders from passing on covenant traditions today?

We may not know the answer to these questions apart from speculation. However, God intervenes for these young men as He does for all of us at various times. He directs Joshua to ensure this new generation of men was circumcised so they would be in alignment with their spiritual heritage before entering battle. This narrative highlights several key lessons about generational influence and responsibility:

1. **Preparation Before Warfare is Key**: Before difficult times come upon us, we need to be in alignment with God. Warriors do not get ready, they stay focused and prepared.

2. **Divine Faithfulness**: God's faithfulness persists even when human commitment wavers. Despite the oversight of their fathers, God appointed Joshua to renew the covenant and ready the people to transition into their destiny (Judges 2, 5).

3. **Intentional Legacy**: It is critical that parents actively transmit spiritual and moral legacies. The neglected rite of circumcision by the children of Israel exposed a significant lapse in their intimacy with God and respect for His covenant. It showcases the repercussions of failing to instill robust faith in our children.

4. **Provision of Leadership**: When parental guidance falls short, God provides alternative mentors and leaders. Joshua's role as a spiritual leader was also pivotal in preparing the next generation to inherit the promise and carry forward the leadership mantle.

This account reveals the necessity of being healed and delivered before one can lead effectively. Parent-leaders may need to address their own past wounds, misconceptions, or shortcomings if they want to be conduits of healing for their children. Legacy-building is more than giving instructions; it involves transformation and a commitment to God's plans to ensure each generation is adequately prepared.

Rites of Passage ceremonies are practical means to facilitate the environment of passing on mantles and building legacies. These ceremonies allow parents and children to reaffirm their oath of love, faith, and family values. They are sacred moments and opportunities to bridge gaps, heal relationships, and intentionally share in generational blessings. Reflecting on this story should prompts us to consider the legacies we are creating in our homes, workplace, and communities. What values and wisdom are we imparting to the next generation?

Mantles are not mics to be dropped; they are legacies to pass on with deliberate care and purpose. Rites of Passage are ceremonies used to implant legacy-sharing in families or communities by uniting people around a central purpose while affirming covenant.

Make It Practical
Before any Rite of Passage event, consider if you have broken places to mend with your children or family members? Are you willing to do what it takes to reconcile?

What tools and resources do you want to pass down for the next generation? Is there an inheritance you want to leave beyond material possessions?

Are there specific life lessons you want to be memorialized in the memories, stories, and conversations about you to future generations of your family?

AFTERWORD

As you reflect on the teachings and stories shared within this Rites of Passage guidebook, you might find yourself seeking additional courage to actively embody these principles. It's time to embrace a bold approach! Your words—spoken and written—and actions carry transformative power over the lives of your children, impacting not only their destinies but also influencing your spouse, coworkers, and friends.

Words wield extraordinary power. Reflect on how Jesus, during his trials in the wilderness, countered every temptation with "It is written." Likewise, God spoke creation into existence, demonstrating that our words partner with unseen forces capable of shaping reality. As bearers of this divine gift, our words are power when they echo God's words.

The Power of a Mother's Words

In preparation for the Rites of Passage Book Release Celebration, I received a profound insight into a mother's words. In scripture, consider the wedding story at Cana in John chapter 2, where Jesus performed His first public miracle. Jesus was prompted by His mother's simple and powerful intervention to help a friend. Her statement to Jesus, "They have no more wine," set the stage for a miraculous act, showcasing her deep faith in God's words and her Son's divine capability.

Mary's actions exemplify the impact of maternal words aligned with God's purpose. She did not doubt or argue when Jesus hesitated to fulfil her request; she simply instructed the servants in the room, "Whatever He says to you, do it." Her total belief in Jesus' identity and potential precipitated the miracle that followed and blessed others. This account highlights how significant the role parents and leaders play in activating faith and encouraging the gifts of those they influence.

The Role of Parent-Leaders in Rites of Passage

As you guide your children or support others through their Rites of Passage journey, consider these foundational principles:

1. **Speak Words of Life**: Your words can set an atmosphere charged with expectation and faith. Declare your children's purpose, strength, and destiny. Teach, correct, and encourage people in your sphere of influence.

2. **Call Forth Greatness**: Like Mary, recognize and call out the potential in your children, even before they see it in themselves. Help others in your family, workplace, and community see their talents as gifts to contribute to the greater good.

3. **Challenge Limitations**: When Jesus expressed concern to his mother, Mary stood her ground and acted in her conviction. Similarly, when your children or those you lead doubt their readiness, it is your faith that can propel them forward.

4. **Teach Through Action**: Mary's instructions to the servants to obey Jesus set a precedent for obedience. She placed an expectation for compliance with her words. Likewise, Rites of Passage events raise the standard and reinforce growth through responsibility, selflessness, and integrity.

5. **Speak the Blessing Intentionally**: The power of blessing others through the Rites of Passage ceremonies cannot be overstated. Bless your children, your family, your community by affirming them to be a world changer right where they are.

6. **Guard your Heart and Watch your Mouth**: Words reflect your inner beliefs and values stored in your soul. Whether it is through kind rebuke or frequent encouragement, your speech shapes the perceptions of those under your leadership.

The Rites of Passage is more than just a ceremonial act; it is an impartation that marks an essential generational transference of grace, wisdom, and courage to uphold the legacy of faith, family, and community.

URGENT CALL TO ACTION FOR PARENTS AND LEADERS

The Rites of Passage ceremonies can empower future leaders—particularly our sons—to stand as men of integrity, fully aware of their identities and ready to embrace their destinies. This guidebook is not meant to be read; it is to be implemented. It is a clarion call to you as parent-leaders and mentors. The legacy you create begins with every word you utter—ensure they embody purpose and intention.

Remember, every leader was once a child, their character molded by the hands of parents and other influential figures. The values instilled, the behaviors demonstrated in private and public, set the foundation for the type of leaders they become. Reflect on the leaders we see today. Who influenced them? What early experiences shaped their leadership style?

It is undeniable that while adults are accountable for their own decisions, the seeds planted in their youth significantly influence their choices later in life. Negative influences can result in flawed leadership characterized by uncontrolled behaviors, entrenched unhealthy patterns, and eroded ethical standards. This fact of life must prompt us as parent-leaders NOT to approach leadership as a role to be assumed when they grow up but as a critical responsibility that begins in childhood and is nurtured as they mature. True leadership is cultivated from the beginning, taught explicitly and absorbed implicitly within the home. If we aspire to raise strong, ethical leaders for tomorrow, our actions today must be deliberate and proactive.

Here's how you contribute as parent-leaders:

1. **Evaluate Yourself** – Reflect on your own character. Are you someone who embodies integrity, humility, and selflessness? Are you the type of leader others aspire to follow? Do you welcome accountability and genuine feedback from others in your space?

2. **Eliminate Counterproductive Behaviors** – Transformation begins with a decision followed by action. The mindset of a leader can either elevate people or be their undoing. Our minds

must be renewed, perspectives challenged, and discipline fostered.

3. **Commit to Continuous Growth and Mentorship** – Never halt your learning journey. Engage in continuous personal development—mentally, physically, spiritually, and emotionally. As you grow, take the opportunity to mentor others, equipping a new generation with the tools to lead effectively.

4. **Pray with Conviction** – Uphold your children, your proteges, and current leaders in prayer. While you may not influence every decision-maker directly, your prayers have the power to reach where you cannot go. Surround the next cadre of leaders with fervent prayer and spiritual support.

As we mature from childhood into adulthood, it's essential to shed the simplistic notions of our youth and embrace the profound responsibilities of fully developed leadership, as aptly noted in 1 Corinthians 13:11: "When I was a child, I spoke and thought and reasoned as a child. But when I grew up, I put away childish things." (NLT)

Let this be the moment you decide to lead by example, setting a course for future generations to follow. Leadership is not about seeking authority or privilege; it's fundamentally about service and sacrifice. It demands a commitment to genuinely care for and serve others, whether within the family, in the workplace, or throughout society. True leadership is rooted deeply in a desire to positively impact others. *Will you rise to this challenge?* The future of our leadership depends on the examples we live today. It begins with your influence, your actions. It starts now.

AUTHOR'S BIOGRAPHY

Sonya D. Ferreira is an award-winning author, speaker, and storyteller whose work centers on moral leadership, principled living, and the sacred responsibility of parents as spiritual leaders. Known for her warm, conversational style, Sonya speaks with the authority and grace of a trusted mentor and the wisdom of a seasoned mother-figure. Her presentations are infused with humor, passion, and a seamless integration of scripture, prayer, and enduring faith.

With heartfelt vulnerability and authenticity, Sonya shares personal stories marked by confessions, fears, triumphs, and leadership transformation—fostering deep and lasting connections with diverse audiences. Her message is legacy-driven, emphasizing the importance of character formation and intergenerational influence in shaping lives over time.

A retired military officer and combat veteran, Sonya brings a unique depth of insight into the challenges faced by military couples and families. Her professional career includes service in civilian and military leadership. As both a writer and a speaker, she masterfully weaves poignant vignettes from her life into powerful lessons, offering guidance and inspiration rooted in real-world experience.

Sonya earned a Master of Arts in Counseling with a specialization in Marriage and Family Therapy from St. Mary's University in San Antonio, Texas, and a Bachelor of Science in Psychology from Bowie State University in Bowie, Maryland. She is married to David, and together they have two sons, Elijah and Ephraim.

EMISSARY WAY

Building bridges of connection and understanding through faith and practical principles

EmissaryWay.com

 Emissary Way

 Emissary Way

 Emissary Way

 Emissary Way

 Emissary Way

www.ingramcontent.com/pod-product-compliance
Lightning Source LLC
Chambersburg PA
CBHW041522120626
46551CB00018B/2534